Cover art courtesy of Serino Coyne

ISBN 978-1-5400-0573-1

WILLIAMSON MUSIC®

EXCLUSIVELY DISTRIBUTED BY
HAL•LEONARD®
7777 W. BLUEMOUND RD. P.O. BOX 13819 MILWAUKEE, WI 53213

In Australia Contact:
Hal Leonard Australia Pty. Ltd.
4 Lentara Court
Cheltenham, Victoria, 3192 Australia
Email: ausadmin@halleonard.com.au

Visit Hal Leonard Online at
www.halleonard.com

BEHIND THE RED DOOR

Music by SCOTT FRANKEL
Lyrics by MICHAEL KORIE

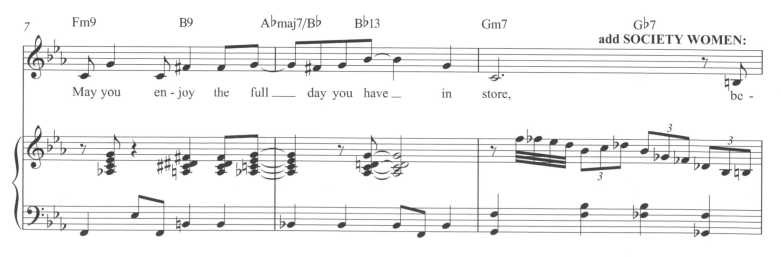

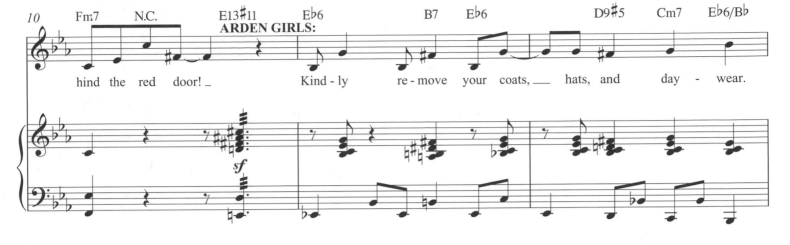

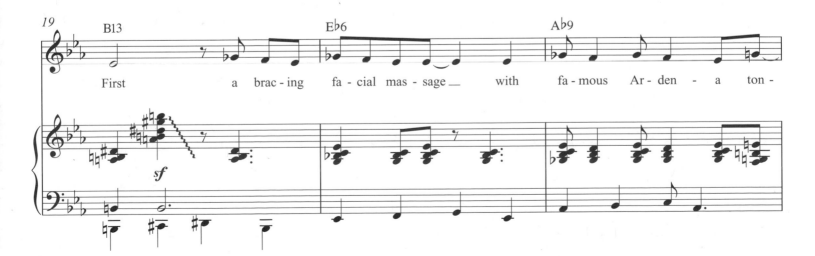

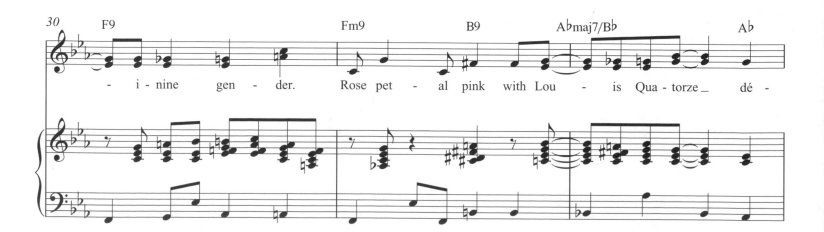

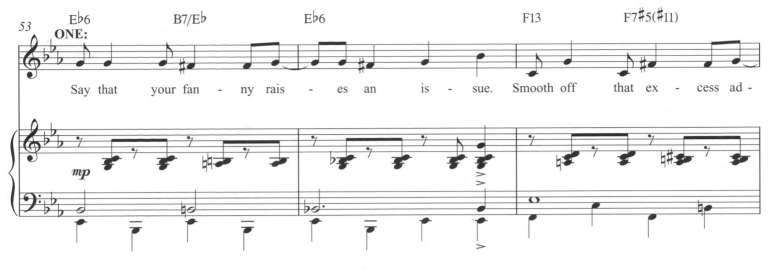

ONE: Say that your fan-ny rais-es an is-sue. Smooth off that ex-cess ad-

ANOTHER: -i-pose tis-sue. That's what the roll-ing glu-te-al press is

ARDEN GIRLS & SOCIETY WOMEN: for, be-hind the red door! ___

straight 8ths

"hurdy gurdy"

ARDEN GIRLS: She's com-ing! She's com-ing! Look bus-y, no slum-ming!

She's round-ing the cor - ner of

East Six - ty - Third! _ She's driv-ing past Tif - fa - ny's

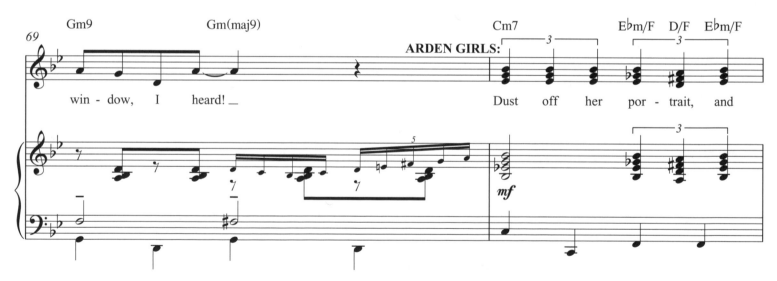

win - dow, I heard! _ Dust off her por - trait, and

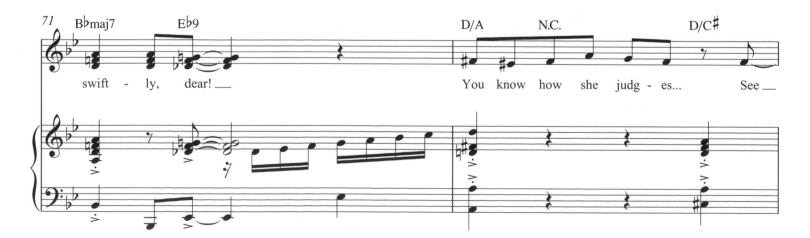

swift - ly, dear! _ You know how she judg - es... See _

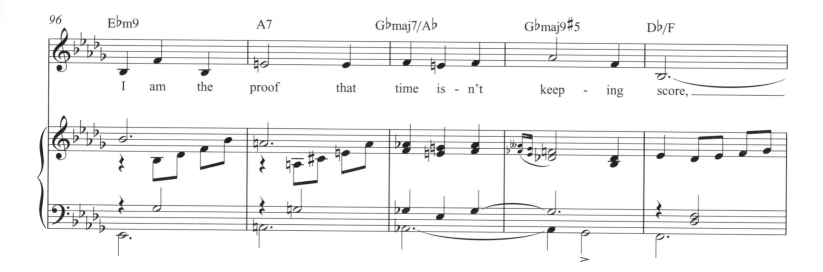

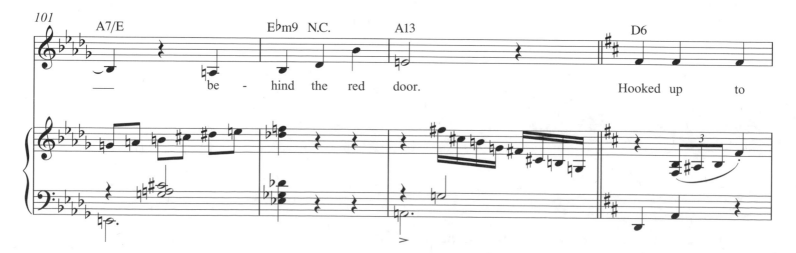

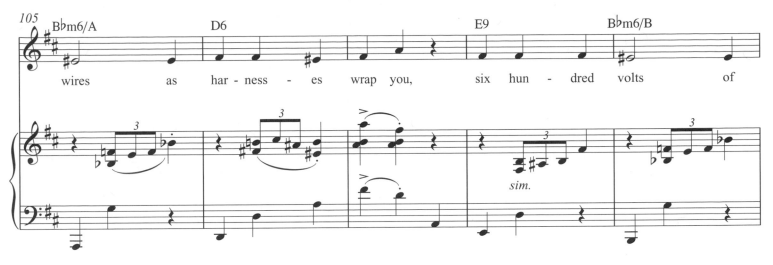

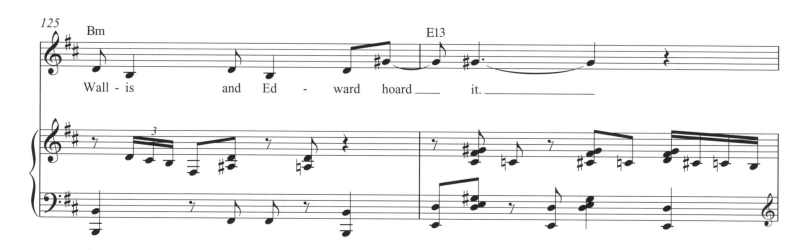

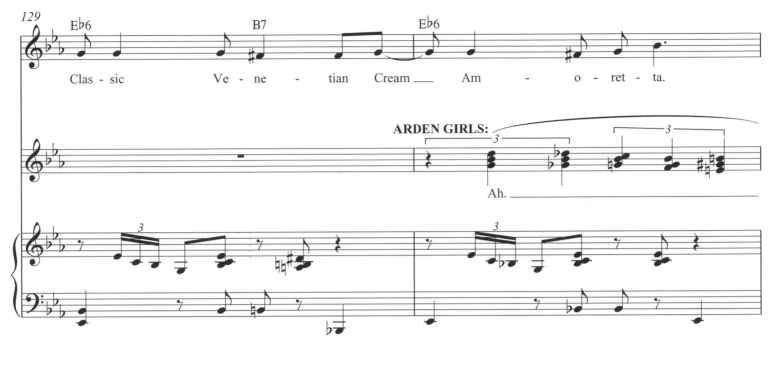

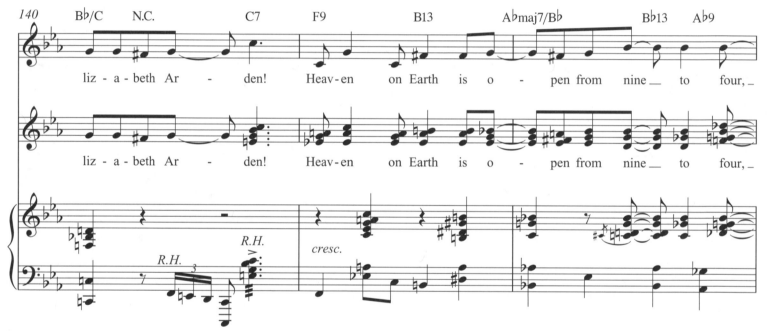

BACK ON TOP

Music by SCOTT FRANKEL
Lyrics by MICHAEL KORIE

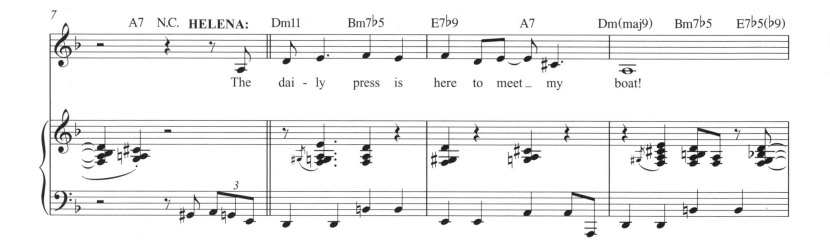

HELENA:
The dai-ly press is here to meet my boat!

There simp-ly are no words, and you may

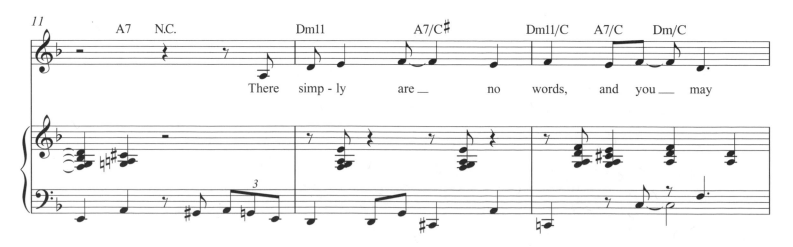

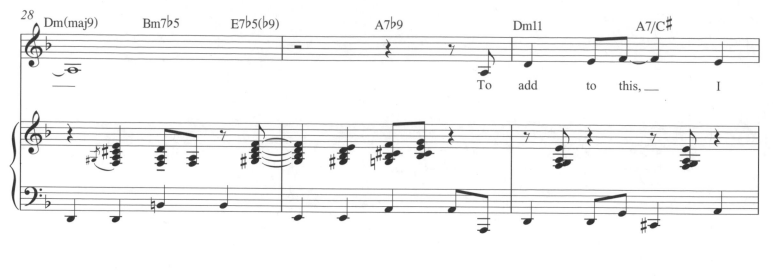

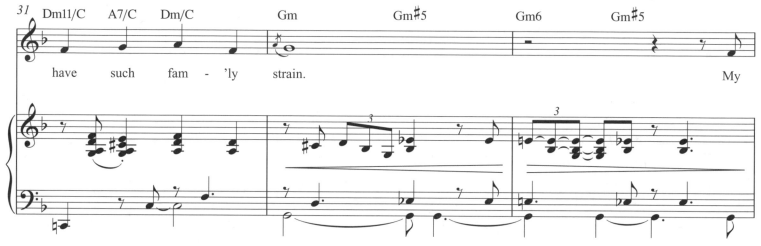

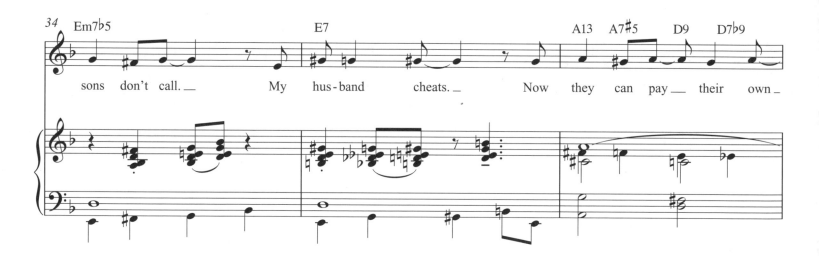

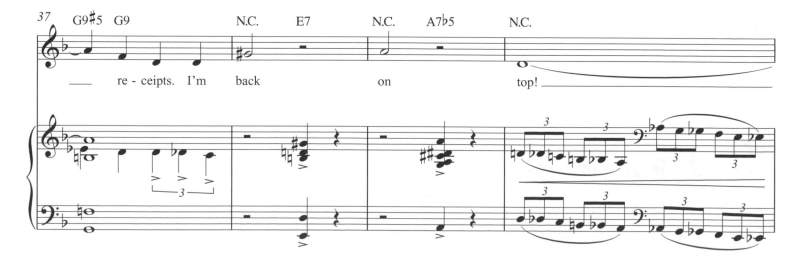

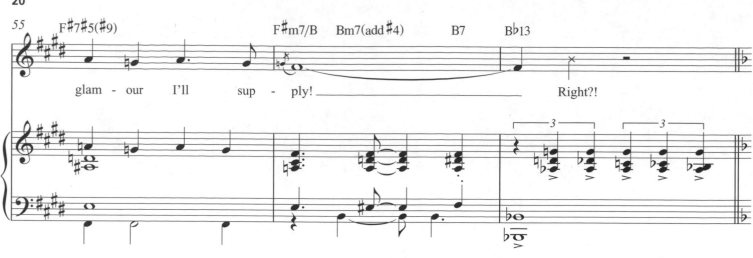

glam - our I'll sup - ply! _____ Right?!

A luck - y thing _ be - fore the Wall _ Street

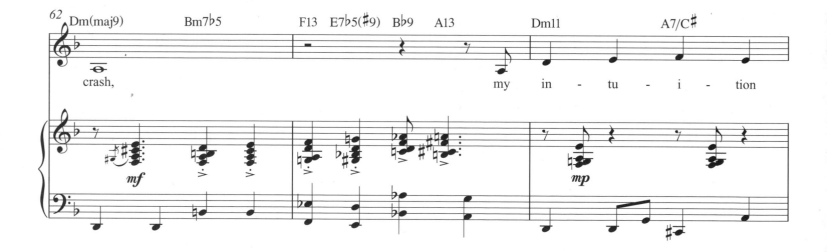

crash, my in - tu - i - tion

told me, "Take the cash." ___ So

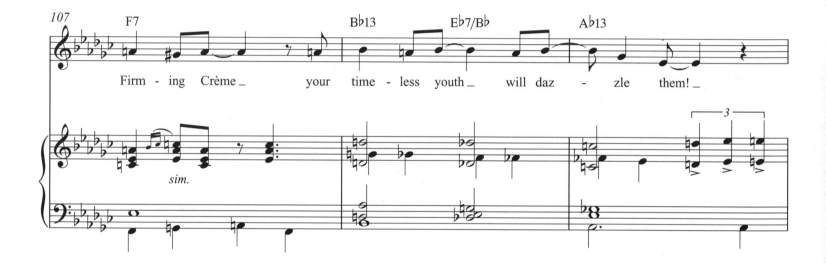

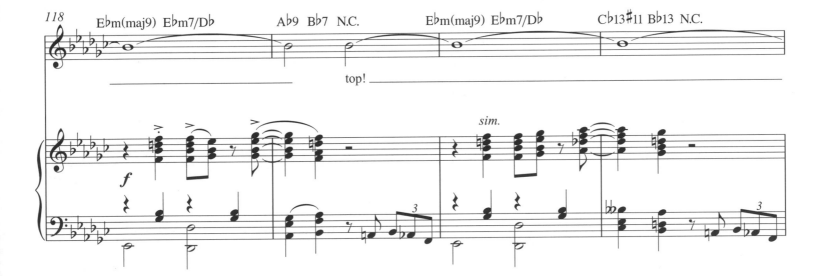

MY AMERICAN MOMENT

Music by SCOTT FRANKEL
Lyrics by MICHAEL KORIE

IF I'D BEEN A MAN

Music by SCOTT FRANKEL
Lyrics by MICHAEL KORIE

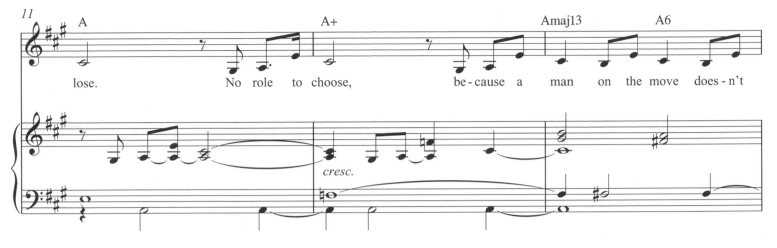

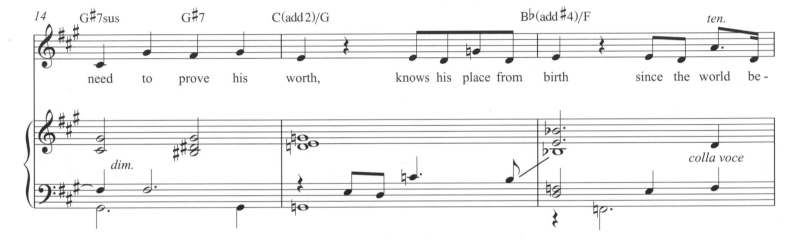

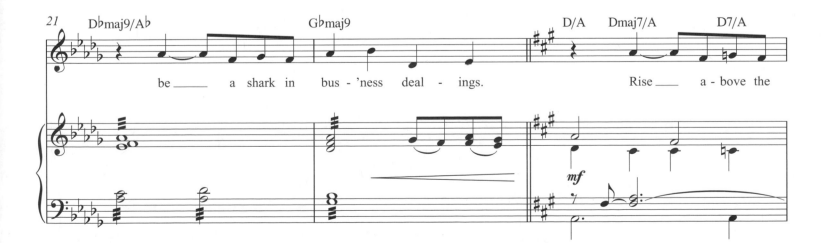

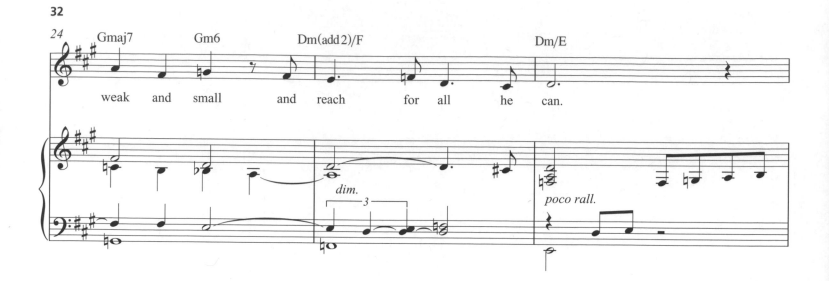

weak and small and reach for all he can.

I _____ a-las am nei-ther ei-ther or. And so my guy walked out the

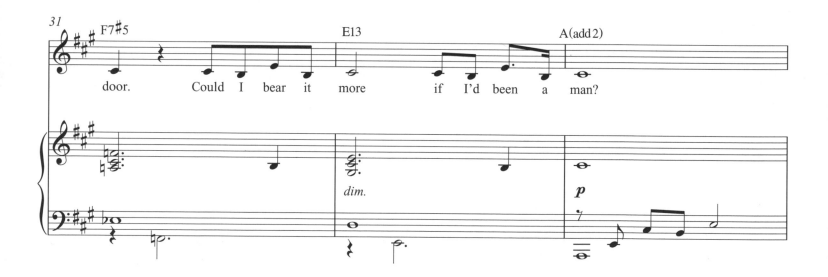

door. Could I bear it more if I'd been a man?

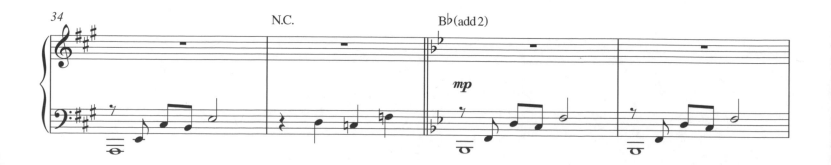

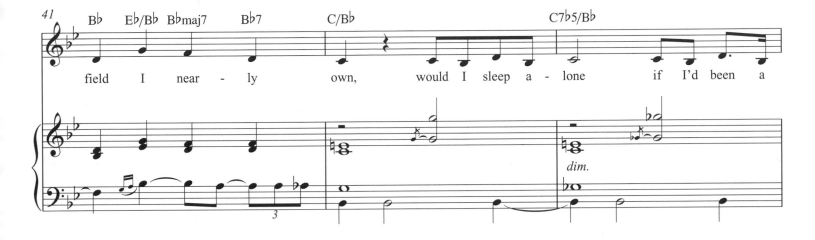

BETTER YOURSELF

Music by SCOTT FRANKEL
Lyrics by MICHAEL KORIE

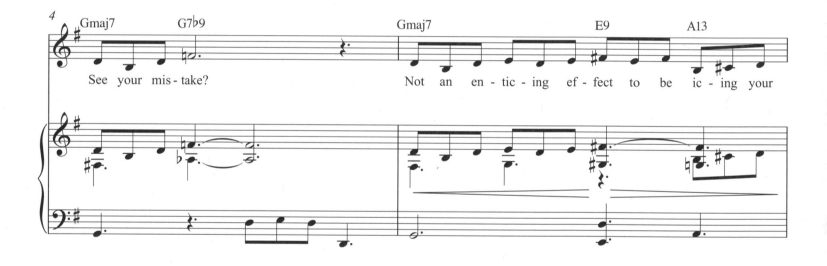

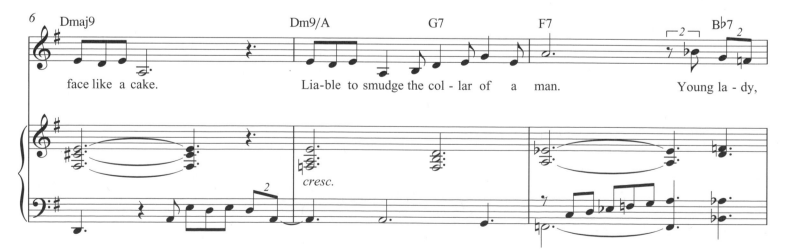

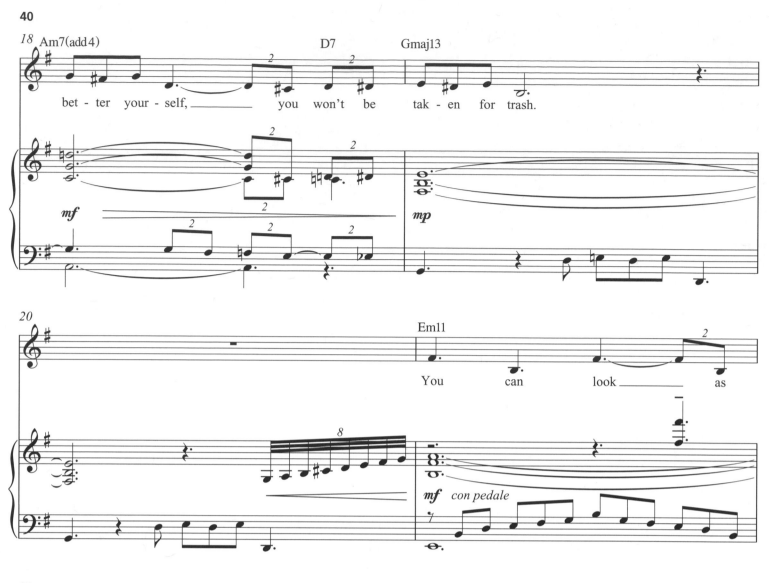

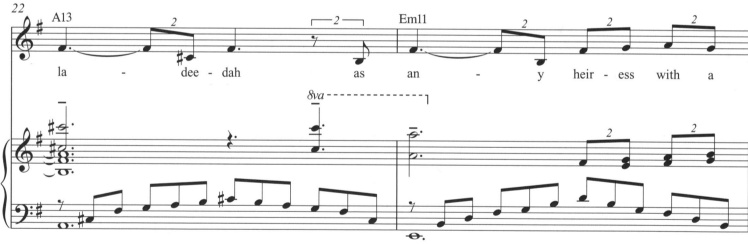

FACE TO FACE

Music by SCOTT FRANKEL
Lyrics by MICHAEL KORIE

Con fuoco (♩ = 108)

HELENA:
Will _____ I ev-er es-cape my shad-ow?

Still _____ at-tached as we al - ways were.

Her, my nem-e-sis and my life - long ri - val.

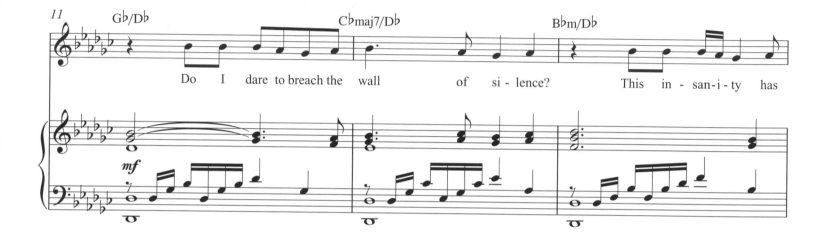

pre - ci - ate my case? Re - veal what's real be -

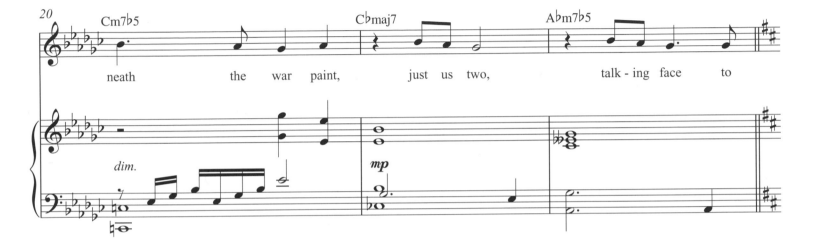

neath the war paint, just us two, talk - ing face to

face.

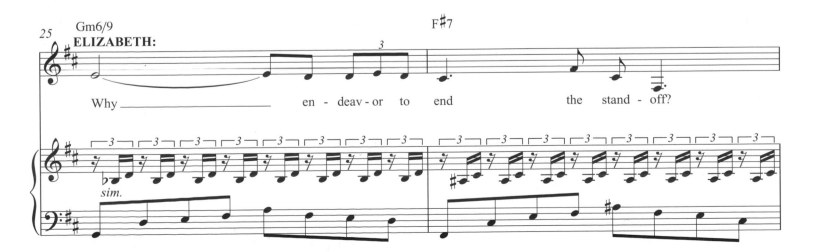

ELIZABETH:

Why _____ en - deav - or to end the stand - off?

I _____ have noth-ing to learn from her.

She, my en-e-my and my would-be e-qual.

Duel-ing ac-tress-es in our "ump-teenth" se-quel.

Though if on-ly we could pool our know-ledge. Make an ar-mi-stice and

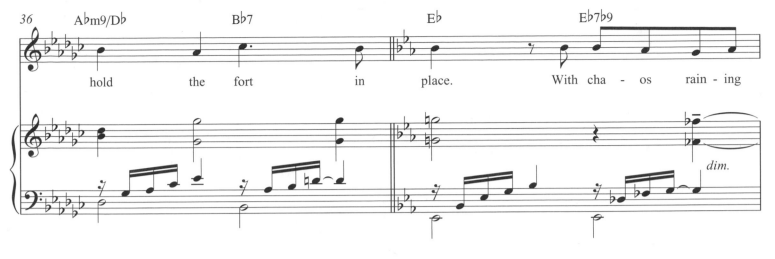

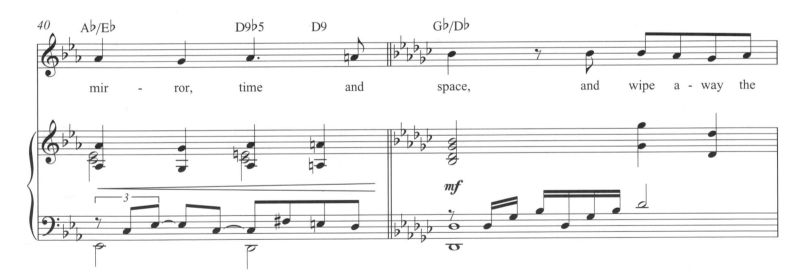

ob - sta - cles life showed me? Or why I moved moun-tains— or

why I crossed o - ceans— or put my am - bi - tions a - bove ___ my e - mo - tions the

day I de - cid - ed I would live the life life owed me! ___

___ Owed *me!* ___ And

Fight u - nit - ed for once in co - ex - ist - ence?

Far too ob - sti - nate to mend our fenc - es,

too com - pet - i - tive to let her win the

race. We cling to our in - stinc - tive grudg - es

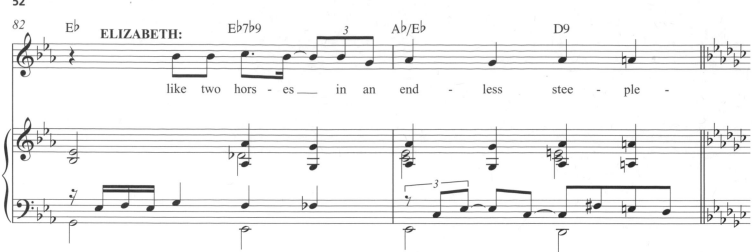

like two hors - es___ in an end - less stee - ple -

chase. Or wipe a - way the mask of make - up?

Just to talk. Not to spar. Man to man. Queen to

queen. On a par, in our fall from

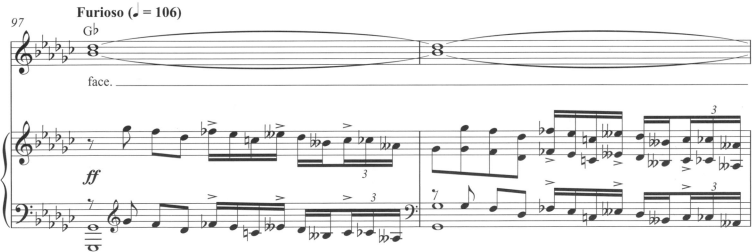

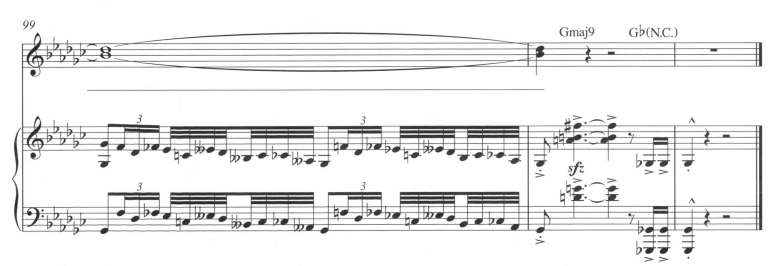

INSIDE OF THE JAR

Music by SCOTT FRANKEL
Lyrics by MICHAEL KORIE

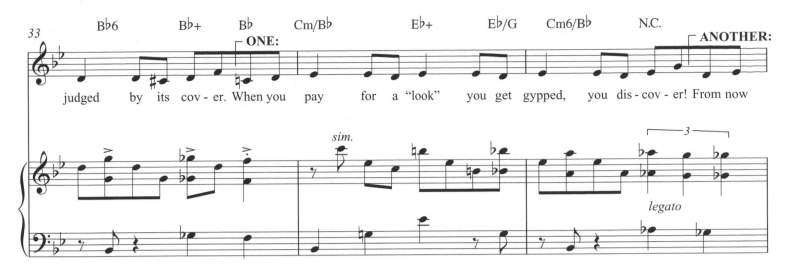

judged by its cov - er. When you pay for a "look" you get gypped, you dis - cov - er! From now

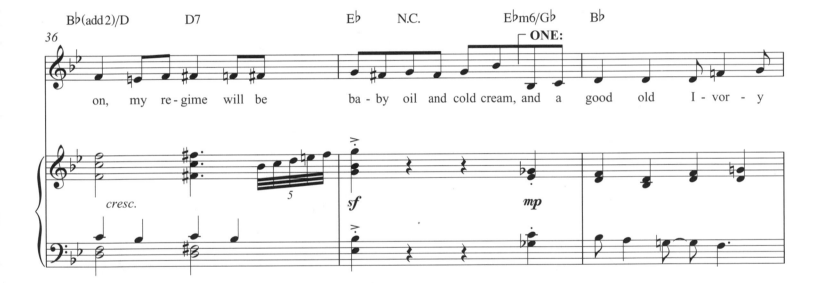

on, my re - gime will be ba - by oil and cold cream, and a good old I - vor - y

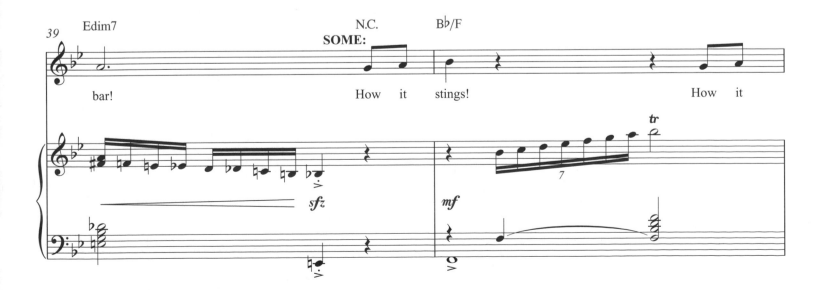

bar! How it stings! How it

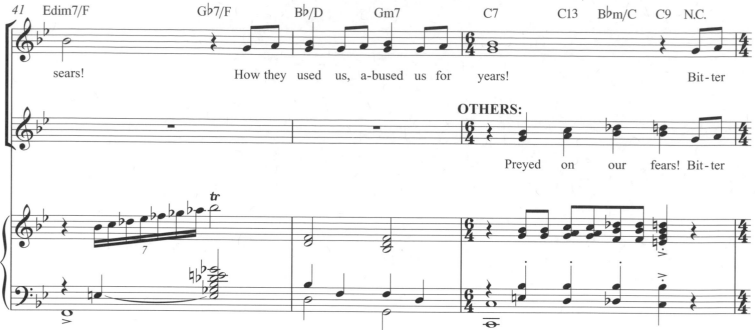

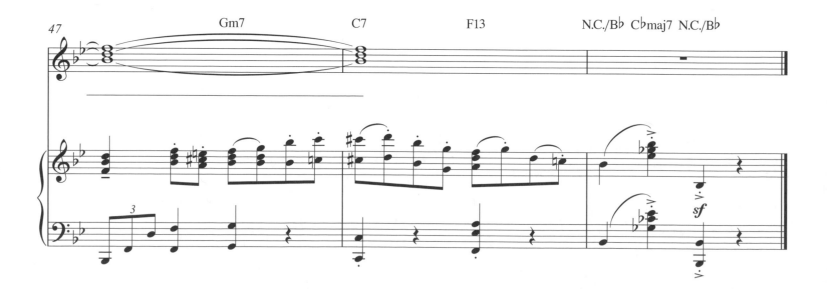

NOW YOU KNOW

Music by SCOTT FRANKEL
Lyrics by MICHAEL KORIE

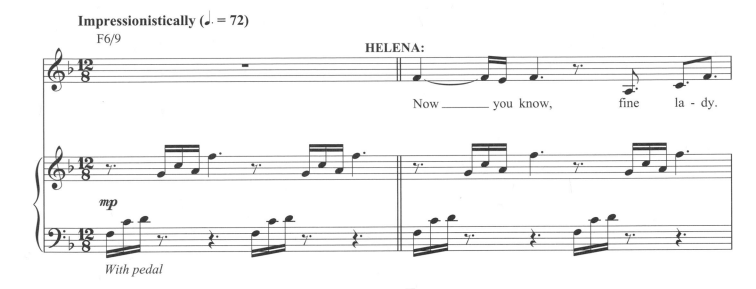

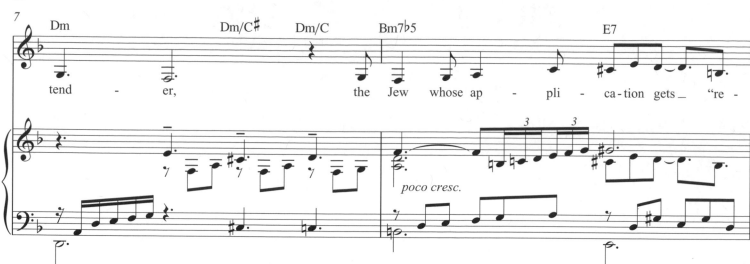

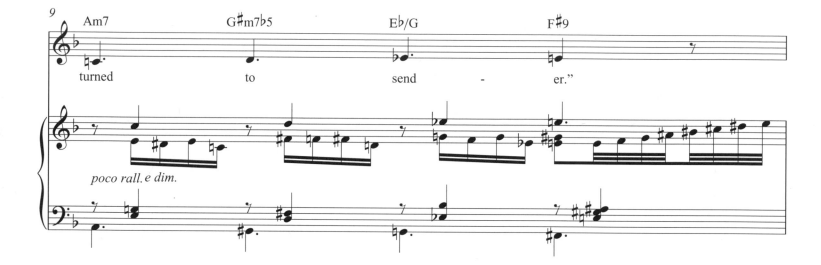

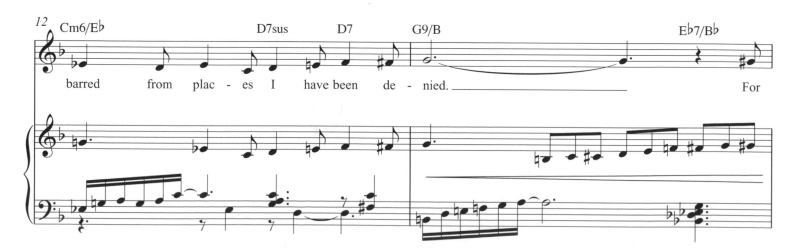

now you know how far _____ from "one of them" _____ you are. And

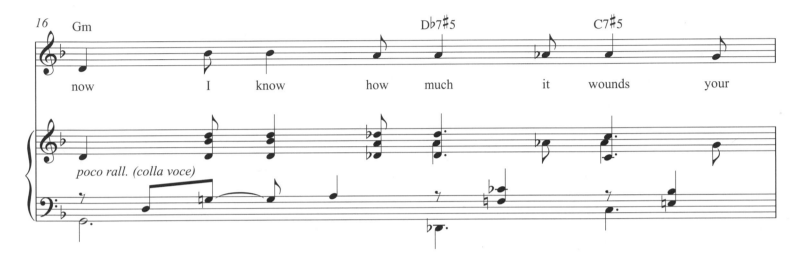

now I know how much it wounds your

pride. You may be fair-er than me, a

good deal blond-er than me, but so-cial-ly they val-ue you__ no

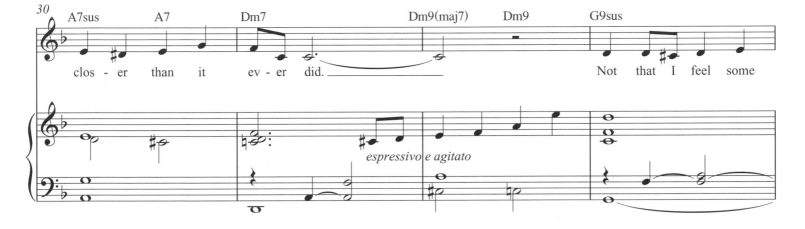

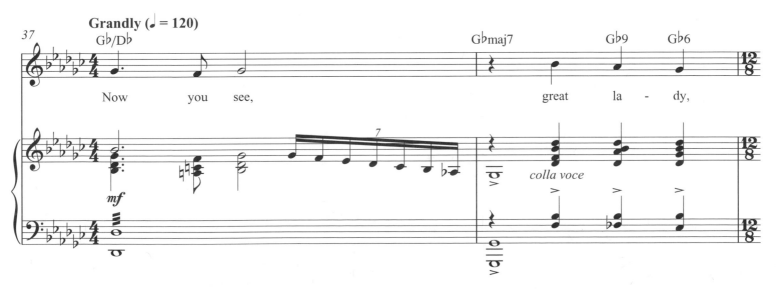

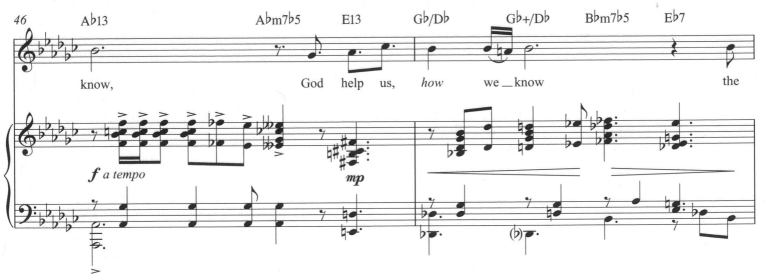

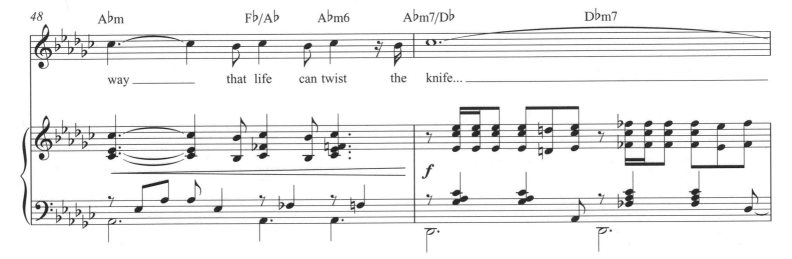

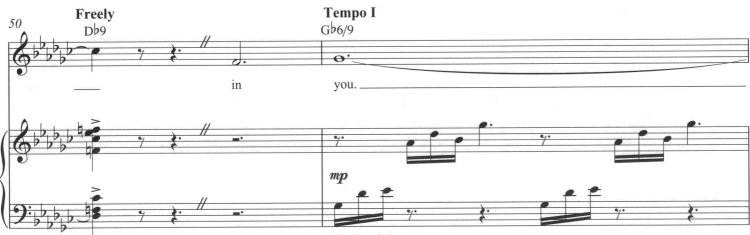

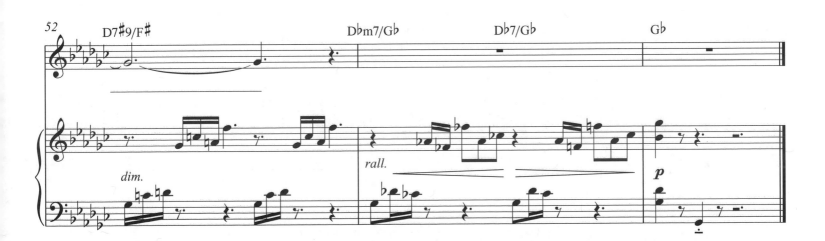

FIRE & ICE

Music by SCOTT FRANKEL
Lyrics by MICHAEL KORIE

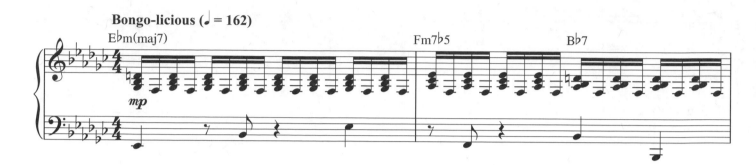

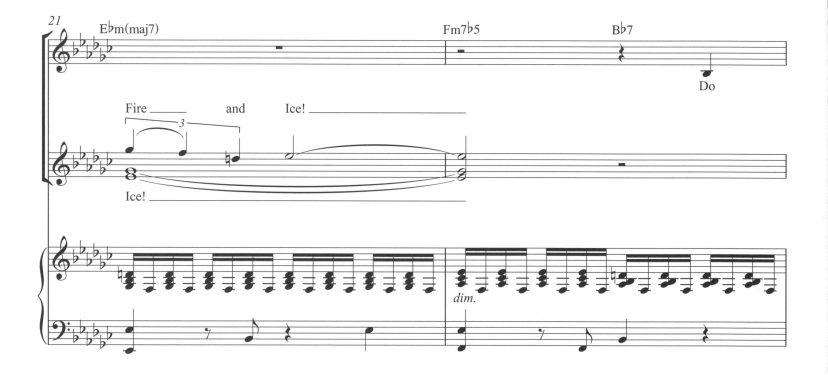

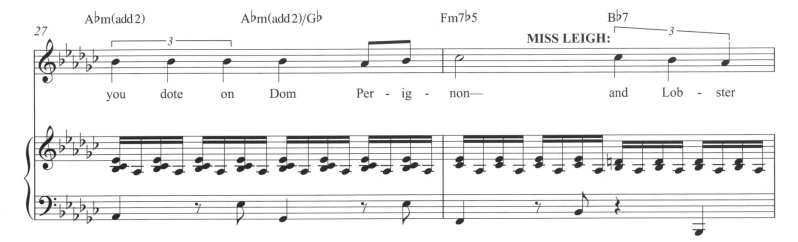

bit - ters, do you like them bet - ter with

two? Do ol - ives a - dorn your mar -

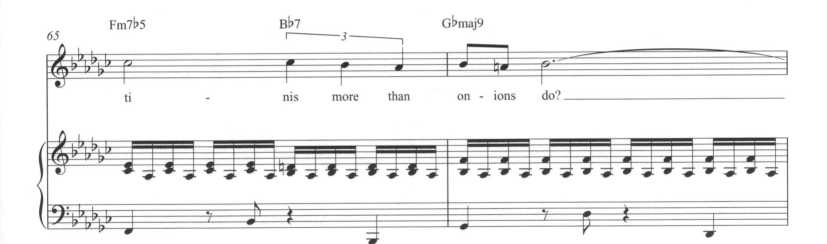

ti - nis more than on - ions do? _____

MISS LEIGH:

Is "pow - er" the scent you

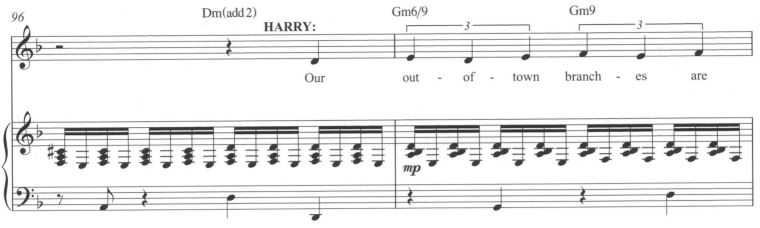

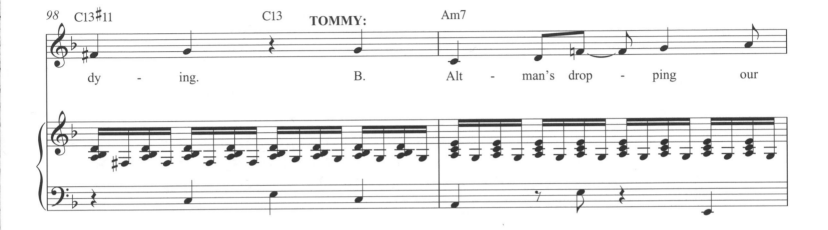

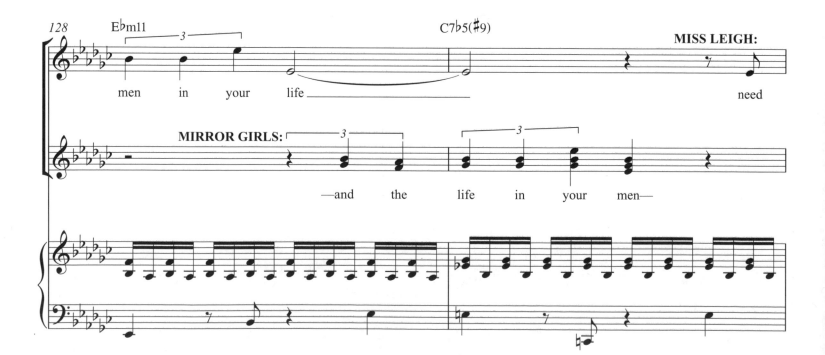

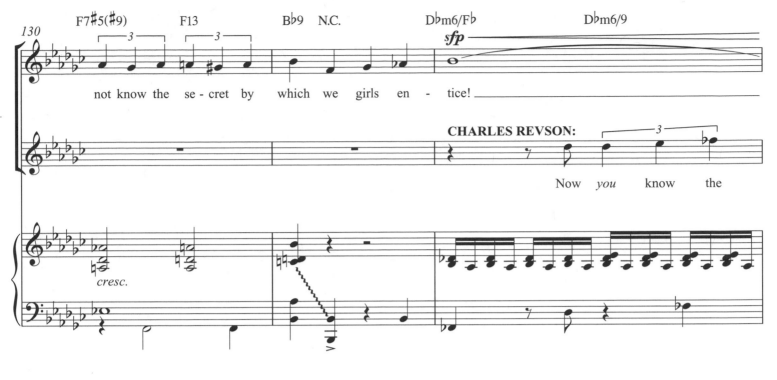

not know the se-cret by which we girls en - tice! ____

CHARLES REVSON:

Now *you* know the

se - cret!

The se - cret be - tween you and

I: ____

DINOSAURS

Music by SCOTT FRANKEL
Lyrics by MICHAEL KORIE

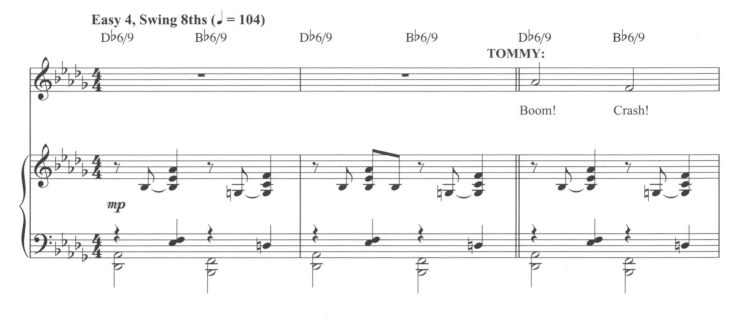

84

PINK

Music by SCOTT FRANKEL
Lyrics by MICHAEL KORIE

More regular

po - sy pink, on Ma - mie Ei - sen - how - er's lips.

Pink on Mrs. __ As - tor's roots and tips. Pink, the box - es

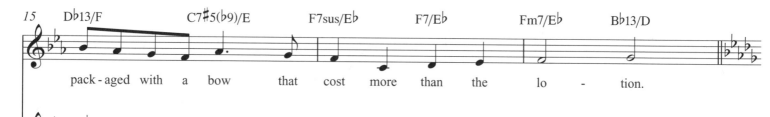

pack - aged with a bow that cost more than the lo - tion.

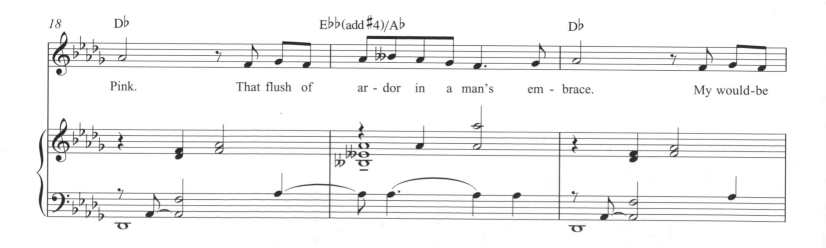

Pink. That flush of ar - dor in a man's em - brace. My would-be

(reads the contract) *The undersigned hereby agrees to license her likeness and trademark color.*

When I was just a farm girl in On-

tar - i - o, could an - y - one have known how far I'd

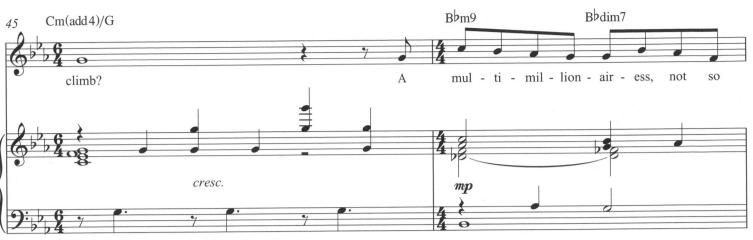

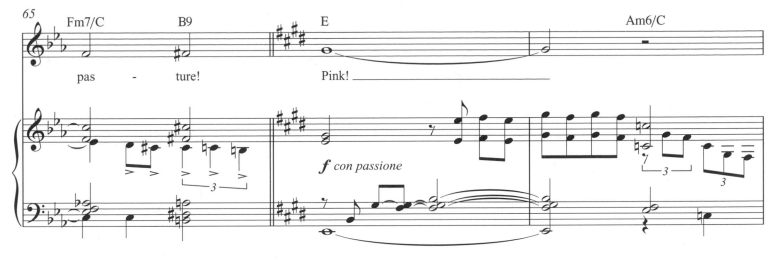

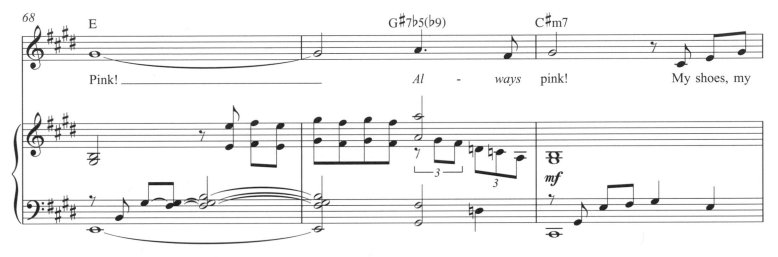

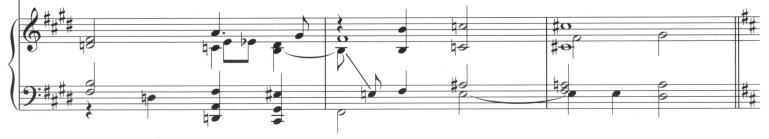

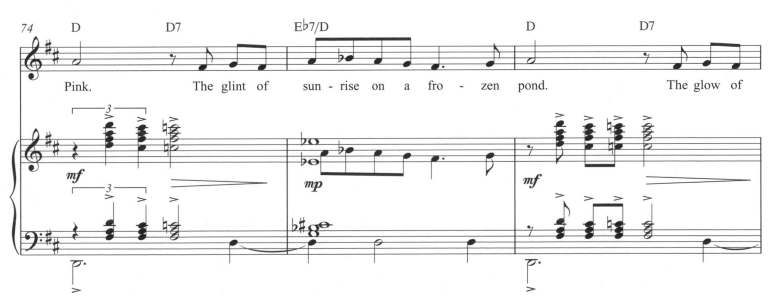

FOREVER BEAUTIFUL

Music by SCOTT FRANKEL
Lyrics by MICHAEL KORIE

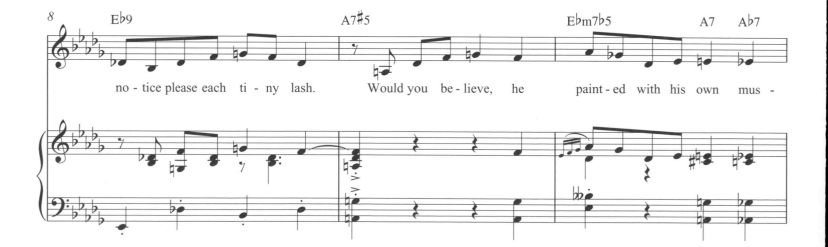

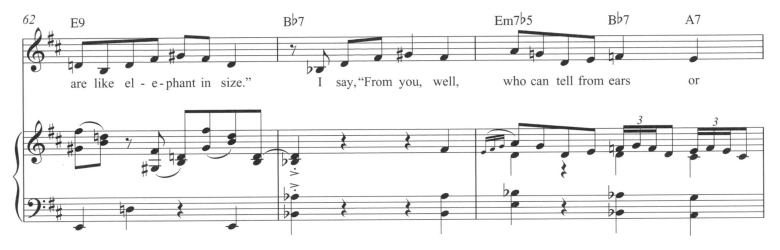

are like el - e - phant in size." I say, "From you, well, who can tell from ears or

eyes?" When I was girl of eight, _____ my pa - pa

sneered at me. A plain - er face he'd nev - er seen be - fore. I said, "To

hell with fate. _____ I'll mold my des - ti - ny." Packed my satch - el and walked right out the

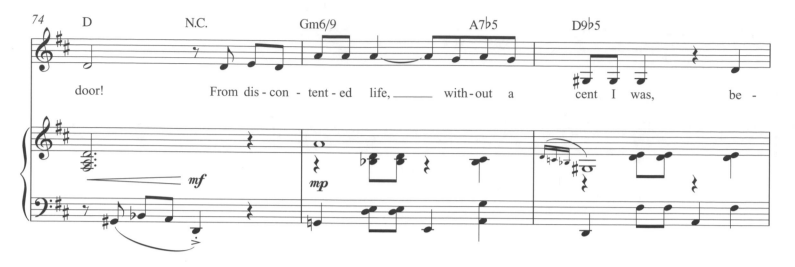

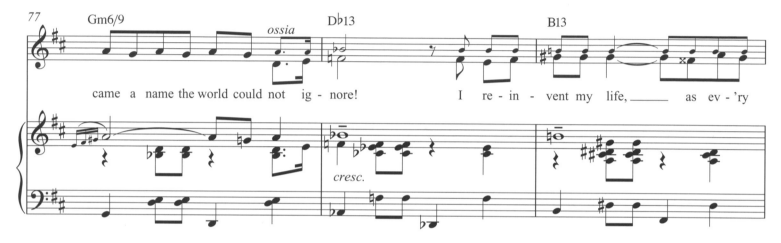

Who says I'm old? I look at my life so far, and I am beau - ti - ful!

And I feel beau - ti - ful! For - ev - er beau - ti - ful! When you feel beau - ti - ful,

you are!

molto rit.

f a tempo

Faster

N.C.

Eb(N.C.)

BEAUTY IN THE WORLD

Music by SCOTT FRANKEL
Lyrics by MICHAEL KORIE

More regular

ELIZABETH: Long be-fore the cir-cus came to town, ev-'ry wom-an's dra-ma __ was her face.

Eyes that glit-tered like a gem, the lov-ers we be-witched with them back then when there was beau-ty in the world.

HELENA: Taste and poise __ were u-ni-ver-sal.

ELIZABETH: Now, it's noise.

HELENA: A dress re-hear-sal.

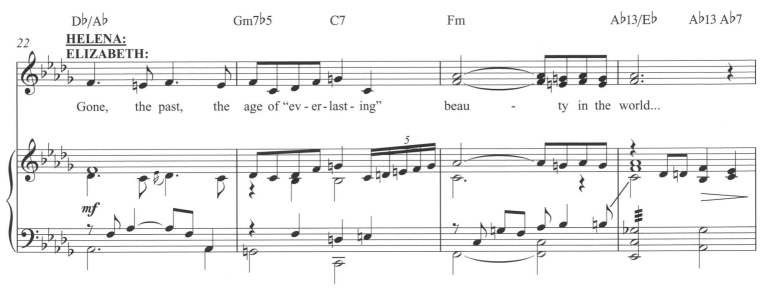

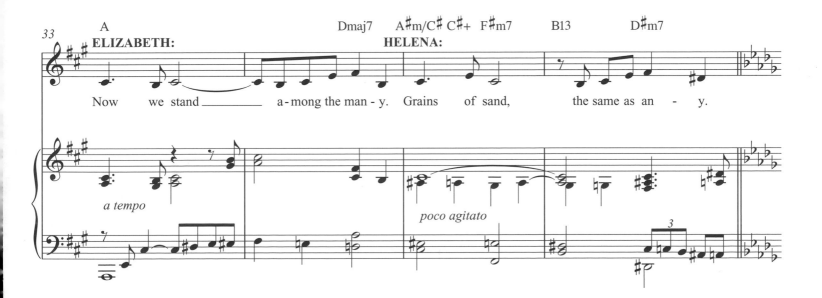